Trapping

Nessa O'Mahony

Nov 07

For
Linda
with warm
good wishes
Nessa

Published by bluechrome publishing 2005

2 4 6 8 10 9 7 5

First published in Great Britain in 2005 by
bluechrome publishing
PO Box 109,
Portishead, Bristol BS20 7ZJ

www.bluechrome.co.uk

A CIP catalogue record for this book is available from the
British Library

ISBN 978-1-904781-70-7

Cover Design © Gwyn Parry

Printed by Biddles Ltd, King's Lynn, Norfolk

Acknowledgements

I would like to thank the following people for their help, insights, intuitive feedback and patient listening during the course of this project: John and Miriam Brennan, Susanne Choudhury, Gillian Clarke, Fiona Curran, Menna Elfyn, Gretel Furner, Michael Healy, Andrew McDonnell, Andrew Motion, Sandeep Parmar, Pauline Plummer, Susan Schreibman, George Szirtes, Carol Thornton, Joseph Woods and Adam Zagajewski. Particular thanks to Carol Rumens for her astute and careful reading of the draft manuscript.

I would also like to thank my parents, Mai and Donal O'Mahony, for their continuing love, support and understanding, and my sister, Finola, for her great kindness in allowing me to stay in her Paris apartment where I completed many of these poems. Finally, I'd like to express my gratitude to the Arts Council of Ireland / An Chomhairle Éalaíon, whose generous financial assistance helped me through the final stages of writing this collection.

Some of these poems have appeared in various magazines and journals, including *Agenda, Breaking The Skin, Coffee House Poetry, Carapace* (South Africa), *Contains Small Parts (UEA Anthology 2003), Electric Acorn, In Media Res* (Canada), *nthposition.com, Orbis, Pelagos* (Italy), *Poetry Ireland Review, Rattalpax* (US), *Skald, Staple, The Clifden Anthology, The Shop, The Stinging Fly, Worm 24.*

I am grateful to Máire Mhac an tSaoí for her permission to publish the translation of her poem, "Oiche Nollaig", to Rita Kelly for her permission to publish the translation of "Bóithre Bána" by Eoghan Ó Tuairisc, to An tUasal Stiofáin Ó hAnnracháin of An Clocomhar Teoranta for his permission to publish the translation of Máirtín Ó Direáin's "An tEarrach Thiar and to the family of Séamas Ó Néill, whose poem "Duilleoga ar an Life" appears here in translation.

Contents

This is how a daughter honours her mother ...
You must peel off your skin, and that of your mother,
and her mother before her. Until there is nothing.
No scar, no skin, no flesh.

Amy Tan, The Joy Luck Club

Section 1

Trapping a Ghost

Waiting for Beelzebub

Each night, listening
for his theme tune,
the sinister tinkle of Tubular Bells.
I'd sniff the air for sulphur,
a drop in temperature,
tensing for the first lift
of bedclothes.

A cold draught:
my back arched,
limbs in spasm.
Dizzy from head-spin,
light from levitation,
my tongue worked,
hissing words I'd heard
in the school-yard.

After it, dead weight,
sleep crawling over me
like flies.

The House of Molaga

at the Franciscan Abbey, Timoleague

In search of one grave,
I found another.
Bony wings spanned
where they'd fallen,
pigeon, dove and hawk
in a mess of feathered ivory;
placed there out of view,
or else drawn to this one spot
where the arc window
shafts light
from the estuary.

Visiting Sylvia

Heptonstall Graveyard, February 2003

Your 40th anniversary.
I'm 40 next year, so I listen to hear
if your bones play chords for daughters.

One who knows you better than me
begins to recite fluently. She's smoother
than the studio-you we listened to last night.

All those *ooo* sounds, raising the ghost of Daddy,
carmined lips blowing smoke rings.
One vowel too many, I'd said.

It seems a poor joke now as we look
at your small heap of granite stones,
the jagged bed for early spring bulbs.

My eyes keep straying to surrounding hills,
the snow's retreat at boundary walls
as if heat of any sort were to be found there.

York child

for Sandeep

A window, small, square,
lattice-striped, set high
in a slant stone wall.
A child's face caught
in the edge of shadow,
staring out each night,
waiting for day
to bring an end to it.

Her night-gown is unchanged;
she's not sure how long
she's worn it, nor when
she last heard her mother's voice.
Sometimes she thinks
she might still be sleeping.

The street is empty,
not even a dog passes, nose down.
The wind blows smoke;
there's a tinge of brown in it
and when she sniffs the air,
she thinks she can smell
the opposite of hunger.

Not that she eats.
There's a weight against the door
she cannot hope to move.
She stares out at winter oaks
fretting the Minster.

Sometimes
she thinks she sees spirits;
crowds passing, looking up, curious.
But they dissolve as the rain falls
and there's nothing
but a crumpled leaf
sweeping the pavement.

A puddle reflects
her face, reflects
the moon:
there's no difference.

Ceres returns for Cemetery Sunday

for my mother

You're more comfortable here
among gravestones,
greeting old friends,
moving through grassy aisles
like a hostess at a garden party.

You make the introductions:
there's Cora Sullivan,
you played with her in Hayden's Yard
the year before you left for boarding school.
She was one of the orchard-raiders
who never got caught ...

Or Dan Murtagh's Ma
who put the fear of god in you,
and so was perpetual target.
You'd pound on her door, then escape
across the green to the grain store.
That's Dan in granite grey;
you flick something
from your eye.

This is the hearth to which we return,
year after year, the last Sunday in July,
cornflowers at the ready.
You point out other displays,
shocked at some new arrival
plump under turned clay.

14

Above a plain slab, an open book
is transcribed with your parents' names
and two of your brothers',
a third brother lies within hailing distance.

The tannoy whines
and the rosary begins.
You murmur glorious mysteries,
secure of your perch
at the edge of the underworld.

Eulogy

In memory of Carmel O'Mahony Campbell

What's left behind ...

you, like a ship of state,
berthed, on view,
our chance to grasp
the last mystery,
to stifle any gasp
at the cold touch of you,
to compose ourselves
as they smooth you
into peacefulness ...

us, like fragments of you:
the same hooked nose,
the bluish tinge under eye,
a sardonic lip curl
when nobody's looking,
the swift cut of hand through air
empress-like as a point's made,
a tone curdling
the innocent remark ...

the words, the scatterings
we'll use in your eulogy,
of a party girl
who knew the recipe
for vodka martinis,
who loved her mother,
who talked dangerously,
who warned us not to go to our graves
without knowing ...

16

who when confined,
charted her whole world
by the phone line,
keeping the rest of us in touch
whether we cared to or not.

Still Life

for my father

You doze, sofa-sprawled,
hands resting
on the gentle rise and fall
of your paunch.
The newspaper open
on the racing page
defies gravity.
Your glasses hang on,
arm tucked in to the neck
of your cardigan.
Your face in repose,
the lines smoothed out,
the Stewart Grainger
hairline intact,
hair still pepper and salt
despite your 77 years.
Shadows beneath your eyes
(the fretwork of blue veins
is a family trait).
Your open mouth
a perfect crescent moon
upturned.
And in that instant
it's my heart that stops.

Love Tokens

They are rectangular slips, flimsy with a week's wear.
Your hand-writing clear, that familiar neatness,
the rounded D I'd trace as a child
when trying to imitate your D.O'M.
Names of winners and losers, starting prices
recalling summer afternoons with Brough Scott and form books.

In the ad breaks, I'd draw horses
frozen in grotesque shapes over Beecher's Brook,
while under breath I'd recite a litany:
Arkle and Pat Taaffe, Midnight Court,
The Minstrel, Mill Reef, Red Rum.

On Saturdays, I'd give you back your chair.
As you watched each race, I'd watch you
rocking on your invisible saddle,
momentum building with every length,
tension coiled, waiting to spring
with joy or a *feck me pink* of torn slips -

much like the ones I'm holding now.
But not as keep-sakes.
My father's daughter,
I'll retrace your steps to Dove Street
and redeem them,
knowing the girl at the desk
will tot them up and never guess their value.

At Saint Lazarian's Holy Well, Old Leighlin

for Kieran Lyons and Michael Brown

Here, hope is the torso of a Barbie doll,
hair yellow-tressing stone.
It is a ventolin inhaler, cap long lost,
gaping its plastic smile.
It is ribbons, knotted and frayed;
purses, skin-wrinkled in red and blue;
hospital cards, dates rain-blotched.
And batteries – remnants
of pace-makers, hearing aids.

It is your lover pulling your collar back,
a quick tear of cloth as a tag, wool mark
and washing guide, is placed on granite.

Lady of letters

In the day my parents' bedroom
was the place where things hid.
Wardrobes were off limits,
crammed full in late November.

The dressing table was always locked,
my mother's riches boxed up,
taken out glittering on nights
when the air was heavy with face powder.

In the chest by her bed, another drawer,
unlocked, easy to creep to
in the half-light of drawn curtains,
dust threatening on its top.

Secreted at the back was my treasure trove,
piles of crinkled cards and letters
next to her supply of writing paper;
I'd feel the blue stock, finger the watermark

then grab a few blank sheets,
listening for sounds downstairs,
take each letter out, learn the shape
of writing, every twist and loop.

Not knowing the sense or sound
but tracing the shape from back to front, page to page,
I matched the curve of ink on my own sheet,
clutching my pen to keep within the lines,

my letters sloping onwards, stalled by ink blotches
where I'd leaned too hard on the nib.
Not faltering at longer words,
I kept the ink flowing.

Tiring, I'd fold the letters up,
return them ill-fitted in their envelopes,
and stash the copies back in my own room,
beneath the mattress where my mother never looked.

Garbally

Wood holds the memory
of this place:

the blackened oak
pulled from a Galway bog
by your brother's friend,
offered without ceremony
on the day of the funeral;

a coffin-lid, makeshift float
some sixty years before,
rafting the older three
down the River Suck,
free-wheeling towards another hiding.

(The last brother told the tale
in the snug afterwards,
cradling his pint,
flicking ash
on the chipped counter.)

Or the amber frame
found in the kitchen press,
trapping a ghost
within fractured glass,
his features your own.

Section II

Writing Slope

Foreword

You came for good when I was seventeen.
The living room was your court
where you taught us how to cheat
at games of whist,
your laugh - half-guffaw, half-chesty cough.

More wolf than grandmother
when we put too much water
in your whiskey glass.
At night, you'd snarl if someone tried
to take your fags away.

Later, there were hospital stays;
your face took on the pallor of the backless gowns
they made you wear.
Once there was a fuss when you lost the radium
they'd plugged you with.

You died.
A good age, we said,
a life well lived,
the pieties expressed
as we cleaned up after funeral guests
and prepared to forget.

Clearing out the spare room
I found your writing slope,
a box in plain wood
too modest to be walnut,
the surface sullen with neglect.

I lifted the lid up.
Beneath, a pile of yellowed scraps,
receipts, old bills.
Then your journal, leather-bound,
the hand-writing faint.
Here and there, newspaper cuttings,
letters, cards
you'd pressed between pages.

At the back, a photo,
sepia and centre-creased:
two figures awkwardly posed,
the formal setting of a studio.
He looked too young for his clothes,
you familiar, with a soft warmth I didn't recognise.

I took the journal out,
turned pages gingerly
lest the spine snap,
drew faded letters
out of envelopes,
read your thoughts,
shook the dust off
a tale you never wanted
to tell the grandchildren.

Up from the sticks

Dublin, 15th August 1919

Dublin!

What a grand word to start this new journal.
Sarah gave it to me as I left,
made me swear to write in it every night -
she knows me too well.

I can't believe I'm here, and, better still,
Kiltimagh is 140 miles away.
The train took forever, all those stops,
boxes thrown on and thrown off,
people coming and going.

But we finally arrived, chugging into Kingsbridge
in a commotion of smoke, whistles and yells.
I kept my head, found the sixpence Father gave me,
told the porter that I'd like a cab.
I think I impressed him with my poise.

Not so the taxi-driver.
He knew of Belgrave Square, but shook his head
when I asked for Mrs Phillips, kept on saying
"But what number house, Miss," in flat Dublin tones.

Then Seán Flood walked by.
I hadn't seen him on the train,
though I'd heard he'd be in Dublin
at the same time.

He saved the day, gave directions
and shared the cab as far as Rathmines Road.
He seemed a gentleman, for all they say.

What a place this is –
wide streets, houses with porticoes,
steps leading up to doors painted in every hue,
brass knockers with lion's heads.

And what gorgeous clothes the women wear!
If Mother got her hands on that stock …

Mrs Phillips just stuck her head around the door –
lights out, apparently. So no more, until tomorrow
when the course begins. Good night, Dublin. Sleep well.

Letter from Father

Aidan Street, Kiltimagh, 2nd September, 1919

My dearest daughter,

I hear from Mrs Phillips that you have arrived
and are settling in well at Belgrave Square.
Treat her with due respect, abide by her rules
and follow her advice on every point.
Never forget you are a Flynn and all that
stands for.

Apply yourself - your mother and I
have sacrificed much to send you.
Máire is making great strides -
she keeps the books and helps
behind the counter on Saturdays.
Sarah says she misses you at the piano.

Be constant with your studies.
I met Mr. Mahaffy the other day;
he said there was great call for secretaries
- there is good money to be earned,
once qualified.

And be regular in your devotions, child.
Monsignor Blake has promised me
he'll tend to your spiritual needs.
He expects to see you at First Friday mass,
the Thursday rosaries, as well as Sundays.
Dublin has temptations enough for the unwary -
let the Church be your guide.

I also hear that young Flood has been to call.
Do not let frivolity
or dubious connections distract you.
That young man runs with a bad crowd.

Your mother asks that you should write to her.
She wishes all the news of Dublin fashion.
Sarah, Máire and the boys send fond regards,
as I do, your loving Father,
William Flynn.

Portrait

Dublin, 15th November 1919

Seán said it would be a grand joke
to pretend we were on honeymoon.
"We'll do it right, all the trimmings,
lunch at Wynns, a stroll through the Green.
We can get our portrait taken in Richmond Street."
He's full of strange notions, that man.

So off we went to lunch
and two of the tastiest cutlets I'd ever had.
We were fierce elegant with our
petit-pois on white porcelain.
The waiter was a Treacy from Enniscrone -
he winked at Seán and kept the wine flowing

so the room tilted when we finally rose
and floated all the way to Richmond Street
to a Georgian house with a smudged brass plate
that said *Greens Photographers.*
We went inside, eyes adjusting to the dark;
the air was heavy with dust and acid smells.

Mr Green was small, he had no time for chat
as he showed us where to stand
next to a large fern in a copper pot.
He took some time arranging us,
fiddling with an oriental screen.
He was ready: "Stand stock still," and we froze,

I thought of Mother and Father,
their portrait gilt-framed over the piano,
imagined where ours might go one day.
Then something flashed,
there was a burning smell,
and it was light and dark at the same time.

Things cleared, Seán paid, and we left,
blinking in the glare of Richmond Street.

Evacuee

Kiltimagh, 30th November 1920

Back home.
I would have stayed
but Dublin wasn't safe.

It was strange, those last days.
The city seemed emptied,
no-one venturing out.
Night after night,
we'd sit with Mrs Phillips,
waiting for news.

If a Castle man was hit,
we knew that meant reprisals;
that somewhere a door
would come crashing down,
men and women dragged out
to God knows where.

Seán joined up,
saying there'd be time enough
to study afterwards.
I didn't care to stay without him.

Kiltimagh seemed so small
when I got off the train,
the houses bare, run-down.
The same old faces,
nothing changed, no-one aware
of the big world beyond Aidan Street.

You couldn't imagine anything
happening here.

New man in town

Kiltimagh, 1ˢᵗ May, 1922

Father heard it in the barber's.

There's a new C.O. at Swinford,
a Breen from Ballina, tough, they say.
He shot a peeler in Newcastle, apparently,
got sent to Parkhurst.

He's supposed to crack down on the Irregulars -
it seems that Dublin's had enough
of all those shows up the mountains,
boys drilling from noon to night,
then rushing through town in armoured cars.

They say Seán's joined them.
It's true he's secretive these days,
and won't explain when he can't meet me.

But I don't understand what this row's about.
We have the Treaty now, and England's beat;
why battle over words?

Tryst

Kiltimagh, June 21st, 1922

The longest day.
The shadows wouldn't lengthen
on the garden wall
and I watched the hall clock
until Father asked if I was expecting someone.
Then nothing but talk, talk, talk at the tea-table;
no-one can speak of anything
but elections and treaties.

Dusk fell and Mother lit the gas-lamps
in the parlour, company was due.
I took my cue, slipping out by the back door.

I waited for an hour.
I wasn't chilled, the air heavy
with heat and the scent of late lilac.
Then Seán came, saying he couldn't stay.

It was a shock to see him in his uniform.
He looked harder, ill at ease.
He said things were tense,
old comrades choosing sides,
wondering which way others would jump.

It's silliness, I said, just a few men
who prefer the feel of a gun,
don't like the thought of going back to ploughs.
He laughed, then promised to meet me on the 23rd.

Later, I crept in through the kitchen door,
Mother and Father still up,
the strains of "Kathleen Mavourneen"
coming from the parlour.

It felt close - I opened the window wide
to let in air, to breathe something other
than dust and songs and get-togethers
and all that talk of dear ould Erin.

Incident at Brady's

Kiltimagh, 23rd June 1922

I can barely write.

It happened this evening.
Mother was pouring tea,
we heard shouts, shots,
people running past,
a woman's scream cutting
through the uproar.
Then a car went speeding
down Main Street.

Father went out, telling us
to keep the doors locked.
It seemed hours waiting for him.

I knew before he said it,
by the way he looked at me.

He said there'd been a row,
a crowd of Irregulars at Brady's Shop.
He said Seán shot Tomás Brady dead,
that Seán had been hurt.

Tomás was in school with me.
He was a gentle soul
and a lovely baritone;
many's the sing-song we had
with Mother and Father.

I keep seeing him lying there,
blood oozing out on the shop floor.

Ah, his poor mother.

But Seán couldn't kill a man.
They must be wrong
but I don't know who to ask.
I daren't go outside
with Father watching me.

I must get word to him.
I pray to God he's alright,
I'll keep praying all night.

Country funeral

Kiltimagh, 28th June, 1922

The burial was today.

Father insisted, saying it was our duty.
I knew the women would look me up and down,
whispering in clusters outside the church:
that's the wan who was walking out with Flood.

The church was thronged, we had to push
to get to the benches at the back,
close to the Little Flower.
One candle was lit beneath her.

I kept my eyes on that,
on the flicker in the red glass,
so I wouldn't have to look
at the altar.

From the front came Mrs Brady's sobs,
so steady and regular
it was like the church taking breaths.
The Latin couldn't drown her out,
the breathing in and out of her tears.

After the gospel, the priest spoke of cruel times,
and didn't we know we shouldn't shelter
those who had turned their faces from God.

He paused, and in that instant
I felt that the congregation had turned
and were staring through me.

I just kept watching the flame,
the red glass flickering,
flickering to a heart-beat
as a woman wept.

On the run

8th July, 1922

My dearest Annie

I'm safe. I can't say where I am,
but I'm being well looked after.
I'm sure that you've been frantic,
listening to all sorts.
I'm hurt, a bullet grazed my side -
but Joe and Barry got me away in time.
The place was swarming within minutes.
Somebody informed, there's always one.

Mick Dolan thinks they can get me out.
If I can reach Belfast and a boat
there'd be someone in New York
to take me in until the fuss dies down.
And when we win, I'll be back.

I can take the pain.
The hardest part, my dear,
is knowing that you are left to face them.
They'll be landing like vultures,
finding out what they can.
Your family will lead the pack.

Don't tell them anything, Nan.
Deny that you've seen me -
you've no idea where I am.
And whatever else, you've no photograph,
nothing that could help them.

And Brady started it -
I was content to finish my pint
but he kept on at us.
If he hadn't bent down -
I thought he was reaching for a gun -
it might have been me
you were reading about.

They're moving me again tonight.
Johnny will get this letter to you –
don't keep it, or if you must, keep it safe.
I'll send for you – just wait, and trust me.
I love you.
Seán.

Martial law

Kiltimagh, 26th July, 1922

More talk in the shop.

Mrs Cunniffe's son is in Western HQ,
and she was in, whispering to Mother.
I tried to look busy with the hat-bands,
straining all the time to hear the news.

Apparently Peadar Brady is up in arms
about the new C.O., Patrick Breen.
It seems the Councillor stormed in,
reading the riot act,
demanding that he raid our house.
Breen refused to take orders
from a civilian.

Brady was beside himself –
didn't he know who he was,
no officer was going to thwart him.
He's writing to the Top Brass,
asking for a reprimand for
"unpatriotic behaviour."

But I'll have to watch myself,
make sure there's nothing to find
if Breen does come to call.

Interrogation

Kiltimagh, 30th August 1922

No word,

but ructions in the house.
Father says I've brought disgrace on them -
he's just worried at what the lads in Brophy's
might say over their balls of malt.
Mother looks at me tearfully,
clutching her rosary beads to her breast.

Captain Breen came to question me.
Gentle-looking, with pale blue eyes.
He spoke quietly, but his questions were hard.
I played dumb, said I hadn't seen Seán in months.
I don't think he believed me −
when he left, he turned and stared at me.

I hate the thought of Seán across the sea.
If he'd just send for me − I'd find the fare.
I can see us both strolling down 5th Avenue,
me in a new straw hat, him looking handsome.
Though I must admit that sometimes
I find it hard to picture him.

I try to imagine the time we last met,
he holds me in his grasp
yet I can't feel his arms around me.
Is that what happens
when two people part?

Billet Doux

Swinford Barracks, 7th May 1923

Dear Miss Flynn,

You will be surprised to hear from me.
I truly hope I caused you no distress
when we last met.
I had my duty to do, no matter how unpleasant.
The thought that I may have given you pain
worried me for a many a day afterwards.
I wanted to write earlier,
but I was in that ambush at Gloir -
a slight wound kept me in hospital.

But I'm recovered and now there's a Truce,
some of us are being let loose in the world
again. I wasn't always a soldier -
before the war I worked with automobiles,
the finest model Ts in Ballina.
It is my plan to find a small space
to work with cars again, to start a business
and a life away from guns.

I'm writing to you because I hope
that you will allow me to call sometime.
I feel badly about the treatment you suffered
and would like the chance to make it up to you.
Please write and let me know
if you might receive me.

Pass on my sincere respects
to your father and mother.
If you wish to reply, please write
to the Barracks - I'll be stationed here
until the end of May.

With warm regards,
Patrick Breen (Capt.)

Second post

Manhattan, 18th September, 1924

My dearest Anne,

Sorry it's been so long.
I haven't had a moment since I got here.
This is a great country - nobody cares
who you are or what side you fought on.
I'm fully fit again and will be moving soon -
I know a man in Philly who promised me a job.
In the meantime I study hard and work part-
time.

It would be great to see you,
but it might be best to wait
until I've got to Philly.
I'll write again soon,   Seán.

Between the lines

Kiltimagh, 20th September 1924

A harmless postcard
waiting for me on the hall table.

There's someone new,
why else
would he tell me to wait?

Now I must stay
in the shade,
behind this counter,

listening to Máire drone,
watching the rust corrode
the bars on the windows,

wipe off the dust
only to see it reappear,
day after day.

Knowing I was his
kept me safe
from the women of the town.

Now they'll measure me up
as I cut their cloth.

Nuptuals

Notice, Western People, 10th June, 1926.

At the Church of the Holy Family, Killeedan,
the marriage of Anne Flynn, daughter of William and Bridget Flynn,
of Aidan Street, Kiltimagh,
to Captain Patrick Breen,
Derrynalacken, Kilfine, Co. Mayo,
late of the Fourth Western Division,
Irish Free State Army.

Anniversary

Ballinasloe, 23ʳᵈ June, 1932

Ten years ago today.

If you had told me then that I'd be sitting here
married to someone else, five kids crawling around,
dishes piled high, nothing but days
of cleaning, washing, cooking,
never knowing where the next month's rent
was coming from, I'd have laughed.

Not much to laugh at.
Pat means well, it's not his fault
he couldn't make a go of the cars.
He suffers badly from that injury.
Not that the country's grateful.
You'd think there'd be something more
for those who fought for Ireland
than the dole or America.

No point in thinking about that.

I catch Pat watching me sometimes
and I'm sharper with him than I mean to be.
Oh god, I'm only 33.

Now Voyager

Ballinasloe, 6ᵗʰ August, 1943

Mary B. was going on about it in Dooley's snug –
the latest thing, she said, with Hollywood's finest,
drooling about that German, what's his name.
I told her she'd be better seeing to her family and feeding her
man, he looks half-starved when he comes in.
But on she went, mouthing about cigarettes
and wanting the moon and some such.
I thought I might just go and see it, sure what harm?

So I found myself snug in the back of the Plaza one-bobs.
Máire was minding the kids, Pat off somewhere.
There was that Betty Davis looking fierce drab,
and the ocean liner and the handsome man,
and the way he lit the cigarettes, two at a time.
It gave me a start, how he handed it to her,
lit, straight from his lips, gentle
like it was the rarest gift he could offer.

That's what Seán did after that Dublin hop.
He walked me home and we stopped
on the corner of Belgrave Square.
"Do you want a smoke?" he asked.
I, never one to admit, said "I do"
and he lit up, held it between his lips,
I could see the red glow of the tip in the dark.
Then he handed it to me, slow like, and I took it in a dream

as if there was nothing else in the world
but that cigarette.
I placed it between my lips and I took a breath in,
as I'd seen my brothers do.
I felt my lungs close over like I was deep in water
and going under for the third time.
I coughed and coughed and he laughed so hard
I thought he'd split himself. 'Take it slow," he said,

so I tried again, breathing easier,
in and out,
in and out,

and I felt light,
like I fitted into the high-
heeled shoes I was wearing.

McAlpine's Fusilier

12th August 1953, Camberwell, London.

My dearest Nan

Enclosed is a draft for £10.
Bring it to Paddy Mack who'll cash it,
that should see you through for a while.
I wish it could be more,
but it's harder than I thought.

The foremen look through me most mornings –
I only get a start if it's someone from home.
Seánie and young Pat are doing fine –
they've got more work than they can handle.
I have to tell them to take it easier.

The digs are grand – a small room
but big enough for the boys and me.
There's hot water between 5 a.m. and 6,
and enough before tea to wash the plaster off.
Mrs B. does a good fry on a Sunday.

On the days I don't work I walk
until the leg starts gipping me,
and there's a good library close by.
Plenty of newspapers so I can keep up

with world events – there's even copies
of the Irish Independent, though days old.
I'm always bumping into some one from home –
is there anyone left over there?

How are the kids? Doing as they're bid, I hope.
They need to work hard, do better than we did.
And what of your news? Write to me, when
there's time.
Was there anyone of note in the Mount?

It won't be long to Christmas.
We'll save enough for the boat and train
to take us back to Ballinasloe in style.
It'll be the best one yet. I promise you, Pat.

Returned Yank

Philadelphia, 20th September, '53.

Dearest Annie,

I wanted to thank you again
for your kindness during my recent trip.
It means a lot to keep in touch
and now that Mom and Dad have passed away,
I feel like you, Pat and the kids
are the only family I have left.

I bet I gave your neighbours a start,
pulling up in the big convertible.
You get used to size in the States
It was bigger, I suppose,
than the ones Pat worked on.
It was a real shame
he couldn't make a go of it.
I guess there wasn't much call.

I don't like the thought of him in England.
I know things are tough
but navvying's for younger men.
I wish you'd let me help -
I've more than enough,
the practice is going well
and there's plenty to spare.
You're family, like I said.

Send some of the boys over.
I could find them a good start.
Think about it.

Give my love to the girls.
I'm glad they liked the candy.
A prettier crop of lassies I never saw -
just like their mother.
With all good wishes,
your old friend, Seán.

Death notice

Ballinasloe, 10th April 1970

The month's mind was today.
The kids came back,
it made the house less empty
though Pat was never a man
to take up much space.

Afterword

Dublin, 20ᵗʰ May, 1987

A small leather pouch
tethered round your neck
with a thong knotted like a rosary.

It hung between your breasts,
a fleshy jewel that had the answer
to life's emergencies.
You'd rummage in it to produce
a crumpled bank-note
when the P.J. Carrolls ran out
or a baby Powers was called for.

You'd never let us see it up close,
turning your cardiganed back
from prying eyes,
clutching the blankets
to your chin.
You kept it with you
in hospital and hospice.

Afterwards,
my mother shook it out
and found a photo,
folded in a small square
which she placed in the journal
in your writing slope.

A photo of you and him –
your faces radiant
as life offered up
its riches.

Section III

Travels and Translations

Muck and ...

When clay was everywhere I dusted myself off,
proud, sure that my habitat was liquid, air,
not bedded in earth, that the clouds
would feed me when I needed nourishment.

I planned for other climates,
packed, unpacked, stacked my principals
in the attic, gave out keepsakes, snaps of me
floating clear and free of territory.

This desert air is bracing, things shift,
the sand slips through my grasp so fast
I barely see its flow, fine particles escape.

I dream of mud-baths, burrowing low
in barrows, digging with clawed fingers
into packed earth, nowhere to go but down.

Fools Gold in Norfolk

Because the words won't flow
I drive through flatlands,
speeding under flat skies until land ends
and sea takes up the slack.
I walk along its edge,
the waves' hiss.
Agates, quartz, obsidians glisten,
tempt my eye to search for amber.
They'll lose their gleam
before I reach the car,
leaving me with pockets full
of sullen geology.

Day Trip to Warham

for Henry Cleverly

A chalk hillside carved centuries ago
so men could watch the sun
and plot destinies by its angle.

I watch it now, my head filling,
the world narrowing
to an acute.

You are beside me.
I sense the need
to turn and look but

the light transfixes me,
the effort too great
to face you.

There's a distant fear;
a shape-shift to something
twitching my tail.

Voices turn inside out,
an empty glass clutched
to breaking point.

The light is too bright
for filtering through semi-circles
of chalky grass.

Somewhere, miles away,
there's me, clamouring
for the dark.

The Power and the Glory

after Pushkin's "Secular Power"

When he was completing his last ritual -
God-made-man dying on the cross -
two women stood beside that ragged tree
frozen in grief. A sinner and a saint,
they shared a name and shared a fate as icons,
two intertwining stems of sin and love.

He's cleaned up nicely. These days
a cross of polished marble sparkles
for the crowds in Phoenix Park
and at its foot, two PR men,
sincere and plausible, adapting facts,
checking legal precedent in their palm pilots.

So tell me, why the need for spin and legalese?
To make media statements out of Holy Writ?
Did you think Christ could do with a make-over?
These days we seek efficiencies when saving souls.
Or had you guessed that your praetorian guard
would turn saints into sinners as they fumbled
in the dark of vestries and dormitories?
That crowds of Marys and Magdalenes
would jostle with their saviour and the press
for a better vantage at the High Court steps?

Leaves on the Liffey

Leaves floating,
brown, silver and red,
tinting the Liffey
as they ride the current.

They spread a green mantle
over the treetops,
over fields and forests,
a long long time ago.

Leaves floating
one misty Autumn day,
carrying beauty
through flooded streets.

Translated from the Gaelic "Duilleoga ar an Life " by Séamas Ó Néill (1910-1981)

Spring in the west

A man scraping clay
off the edge of his spade
in the fragile quiet
of the midday heat:
    sweet the sound
      of spring in the west.

A man throwing
a creel from his back,
red seaweed
glistening
in the sunshine
on the white shingle beach:
    splendid the sight
      of spring in the west.

Women in the rock pools
at low tide,
their frocks tucked up,
shadows beneath them:
    a sight to ease you,
      spring in the west.

Stiff-buttocked rowers
oars gently stroking,
the currach loaded
heading for shore
slow over marigold neap tide
at the end of day;
    spring in the west.

Translated from the Gaelic "An tEarrach Thiar" by Máirtín Ó Direáin (1910-1988)

White Roads

I'm far from the roads,
those long roads, sun-bleached,
winding westward beyond the plain,
lazily loitering their way astray.

Memory wails its loneliness:
I hear the snipe's sharp stilletto
cutting through the bog's silence,
disturbing the dreams of the dead.

A pensive black donkey
reckoning every footfall on his journey,
a tall girl with regal legs
draws water in her little pail.

The village sleeps
smoke rising in straight lines,
each door offering shelter,
the sweet smell of booze in the heat of the day.

The road winds westwards again,
gold melting on the treetops,
sweet drunkenness in the afternoon,
the world bewitched by a bird's poetry.

I'm far from those roads,
the sun-bleached roads,
and my memory wanders off with them
away from the city's clamour.

Translated from the Gaelic "Bóithre Bána" by Eoghan Ó Tuairisc (1919-1982).

Christmas Eve

The sky is speckled with angel light,
frost gives bite to the mountain wind,
so kindle the fire and go to bed,
the Christ Child will sleep in this house tonight.

Leave the door open for the guests we expect,
a virgin and the infant she carries at her breast,
take your ease from the weary road, a stór,
Let the Christ Child sleep in this house tonight.

The lights shone bright in that lodging-house,
cosy with comfort, with food and with drink,
decked with merchants' wool and silk,
but the Christ Child will sleep in this house tonight.

Translated from the Gaelic "Oiche Nollaig" by Máire Mhac an tSaoí

Venice postcards

1. At the Peggy Guggenheim

Riveted by a boy again,
equestrian this time, bronze,
erection pointing canal-wards
sign-posting the end
of this pilgrimage
through a dilettante's garden -
who wouldn't choose
to be buried with their art
and 14 shih-tzus?

2. School Outing

They've come straight from Grafton Street
to the Riva, voices shrill, dodging dames in furs.
They rush, fuelled by something sneaked
between gondola rides and secret tours,

panicking mid the tri-corn hats,
clutching bags, fleeing the Carnivale,
they clatter on, dropping cameras,
a compact bought in Boots.

Till they're brought up short,
energy corralled by the gate-keeper
who waits for them at the water's edge
foot tapping, lips pursed.

Santa Salute chimes the lock-up bell.

3. On the gondola

It might have been romantic
if we'd both brought someone else,
so we settled for self-consciousness,
admiring Roberto's spiel and Roberto's ass.

No hand-trailing here,
but languidness all the same
being propelled through the *calle*
hearing the water lap, the plop
of plaster crumbling,
a rat swimming somewhere.

Agristi Express

1. Cyber café

Hazy, the Greek sky veiling itself.
The radio knock knocking
on heaven's door at the Sunrise,
where I'm the only customer.
The espresso's good
and a Marley loop
blares round this island time forgot
save for stragglers,
brown-skinned, wrinkled voyagers
on Vespas and fishing boats.
They're kings of the hill, three towns,
an hourly ferry (though not in the afternoon),
dust, holes, pipes leading nowhere.
Up at Milos, the church is a closed white square,
its gold hidden through browned glass,
the glitter of silver foil.
A single eye stares out,
deflecting evil onto malcontents.

2. *Aegean*

Blue, blue day,
aqua, ultramarine,
indigo, turquoise, cobalt,
colours seeping in a wash
till the eye can't take it in.
Feel it enter skin, run
vein deep.

3. Holiday weekend

The island waits
for the lover who promises much.
She waits, bedecked,
tidying away dust
under pavements,
painting steps to the cove
blue and white,
covering cracks,
baking bread.
He'll take his fill,
sit up all night carousing,
sleep late, a grumbling
tousled head emerging
behind curtains
in time for the last boat,
scrambling down the hill.
Laughter the last thing she'll hear
in the ship's wake.

4. Balcony at Rosie's

From here you can decide
what it's all about:
what's said, the banter
over butter, whether jam
or honey is the perfect blend
with yoghurt you can stand a spoon in.
Tasks are set, an exercise
in taking your time,
hearing your breath,
learning to come to terms,
how to make a place
among cicadas and dust and cobalt seas
and day-trippers trudging
pasty-faced from the harbour.
The cat seems sure, kissing
the path with delicate pads,
holding you in her almond gaze,
teasing you with the answer.

24, rue de Cotte

for Finola O'Mahony

You depart in a whirl
of last minutes -
reminders of what to do,
of where to put myself.
Then you're gone, leaving me
to climb the four flights,
the ancient wood curving into itself,
held intact by two centuries of footfalls.
My feet must make adjustments,
to the climb,
to the six-sided floor tiles
in your apartment.
I'm still slipping,
and though you're not here
to pick me up,
I feel you in the mint walls;
the four roses drooping
after a night on the town;
the champagne stock-piled;
the sibilant hiss of
TSF jazz radio.
And in that family shot
- you're the only one
not looking at the camera -
keeping a benign eye
on la petite soeur.

Modern romance

I turn to mood music,
all that talk of boy-girl
buzzing in my head.
A matter of technique, you'd said,
erogenous zones,
and had I never?

I turn the jazz up,
stretch out.
My fingers,
nervous on their first date,
fumble, stroke,
get bored.

Not trying hard enough.

I watch the swallows
carving up the dusk.
I strive to match their movements,
fail,
kneading bread
with a blunt instrument.

Echoes next door;
a pair caterwaul
their passion ...

the tenor sax moans.

Home thoughts

Why am I thinking of you tonight
when it's been years?
Why am I feeling it now,
here, in another country,
suddenly distracted by
the way your hand parted me,
slipping in as if
you were just returning home,
the look of remembering,
that dreamy, certain look
as your hand curved me,
split me into segments?
And why am I thinking of it now,
when it's been years,
and I'm whole now,
and in another country,
when there's no need of parting,
of wanting to be half?

Hit Delete

I remove you from the address-book,
my cursor swipe sideways
wipes any trace of you.

Next to the inbox,
your messages
a right click away
from obliteration.

I pause, thinking how years ago
I might have gathered them up,
damp from maiden's tears,
and wrapped them, beribboned
into a box destined for dust
and the top shelf.

No, I prefer erasure,
the steely composure
of thumb and index,
as I make my mouse
roar.

To the Muse

I stopped believing ...

    in Santa Claus at seven,
    the tooth fairy at nine,
    the Catholic church at seventeen,
    paternal infallibility at twenty-two,
    Mr Right at thirty-seven.

Now give me one good reason ...

A writer's life

I get to the Ferlinghetti part
but my eye keeps drifting
from the print to the tiled floor.
There's powder crystalised around a cigarette-butt
and a large madame checking the séchoir[1],
rippling the air as she shakes out sheets
she folds into huge squares.

To my left, the thumping swirl,
a constant spin of towels and underwear.
A black sock becomes for an instant
an agonised L pinned against glass,
then disappears into the vortex.

---

[1] French tumble-dryer

Alternative role models for the Irish poet

for Adam Zagajewski

Yeats and Kavanagh in a tea-room.
Willie is all angles, pinkie cocked
over crockery.
He toys with cucumber fingers
not quite the standard of Lissadell,
chants the menu for the puzzled room.
Paddy ignores the food,
slurps tea out of the saucer,
spud-gnarled thumbs fumbling
with the porcelain as he looks around
for enemies.

Outside, a mechanical songbird
balances on a wire; its thrilling notes drown
a bedraggled sparrow's cheep.

Biography

Nessa O'Mahony was born in Dublin in 1964. Her poetry has appeared in a number of Irish, UK and North American periodicals including *Poetry Ireland Review*, *The Shop*, *nthpositon.com*, *The Stinging Fly*, *Agenda*, *Orbis*, *Staple*, *In Media Res* (Canada), and the *Atlanta Review* and has also been broadcast by RTÉ radio. Her first poetry collection, entitled *"Bar Talk"*, was published by *iTaLiCs Press* in Dublin in 1999. She is editor of the online literary magazine, Electric Acorn (*http://acorn.dublinwriters.org*). She completed an MA in Creative Writing at the University of East Anglia in 2003 and is now undertaking a PhD in Creative Writing at the University of Wales, Bangor. She was awarded a literature bursary by the Arts Council of Ireland / An Chomhairle Éalaíon in 2004.